Ned in Bed

and

Fun at the Park

By
Jill Atkins

Illustrated by
Jordan Wray

The Letter B

Trace the lower and upper case letter with a finger. Sound out the letter.

Down,
up,
around

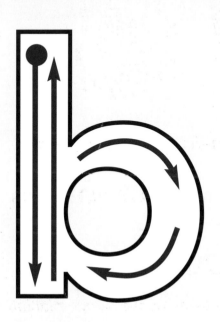

Down,
up,
around,
around

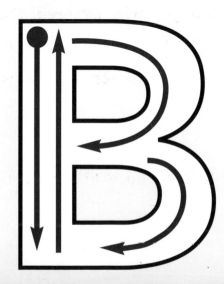

Ned in Bed

and

Fun at the Park

Th

T!
a f.

Maverick
Early Readers

'Ned in Bed' and 'Fun at the Park'
An original concept by Jill Atkins
© Jill Atkins

Illustrated by Jordan Wray

Published by MAVERICK ARTS PUBLISHING LTD
Studio 3A, City Business Centre, 6 Brighton Road,
Horsham, West Sussex, RH13 5BB
© Maverick Arts Publishing Limited July 2017
+44 (0)1403 256941

A CIP catalogue record for this book is available at the British Library.

ISBN 978-1-84886-285-2

www.maverickbooks.co.uk

This book is rated as: Pink Band (Guided Reading)
This story is decodable at Letters and Sounds Phase 2.

Some words to familiarise:

Ned rabbit fell

High-frequency words:

got in a out of oh no

Tips for Reading 'Ned in Bed'

- Practise the words listed above before reading the story.
- If the reader struggles with any of the other words, ask them to look for sounds they know in the word. Encourage them to sound out the words and help them read the words if necessary.
- After reading the story, ask the reader why Ned fell out of bed.

Fun Activity

Discuss why the animals may want to sleep in Ned's bed.

Ned in Bed

Ned got in bed.

A duck got in bed.

A rabbit got in bed.

A cat got in bed.

A dog got in bed.

Ned fell out of bed!

The Letter U

Trace the lower and upper case letter with a finger. Sound out the letter.

*Down,
around,
up,
down*

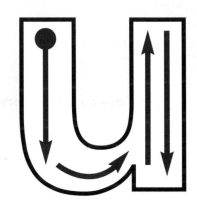

*Down,
around,
up*

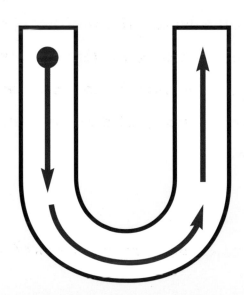

Some words to familiarise:

Sid   down   Gus

High-frequency words:

can   go   up

Tips for Reading 'Fun at the Park'

- Practise the words listed above before reading the story.
- If the reader struggles with any of the other words, ask them to look for sounds they know in the word. Encourage them to sound out the words and help them read the words if necessary.
- After reading the story, ask the reader why Kim and Tim are going up and down.

Fun Activity

What other ways can you go up and down?

Fun at the Park

Sid can go up.

Sid can go down.

Bess can go up.

Bess can go down.

Gus can go up.

Gus can go down.

Kim can go up.

Tim can go down.

Book Bands for Guided Reading

The Institute of Education book banding system is a scale of colours that reflects the various levels of reading difficulty. The bands are assigned by taking into account the content, the language style, the layout and phonics.

Maverick Early Readers are a bright, attractive range of books covering the pink to purple bands. All of these books have been book banded for guided reading to the industry standard and edited by a leading educational consultant.

For more titles visit:
www.maverickbooks.co.uk/early-readers

 Pink

 Red

 Yellow

 Blue

 Green

 Orange

 Turquoise

 Purple

Book Band Pink

Bad Dog and No, Nell, No!	978-1-84886-287-6
Meg and Rat and Puff! Puff! Puff!	978-1-84886-286-9
Ned in Bed and Fun at the Park	978-1-84886-285-2
Cool Duck and Lots of Hats	978-1-84886-249-4
Peck, Hen, Peck! and Ben's Pet	978-1-84886-248-7